The Wooden Gate

Brendan Doyle

The Wooden Gate

Acknowledgements

Poems in this collection have previously been published in
Eureka Street
Australian Poetry Journal
Australian Poetry Anthology 2015
and *First Refuge: poems on social justice* (Ginninderra Press)

Dedication

This collection is dedicated to the memory of my parents
and my sister Marion.

With gratitude to Deb Westbury and Vanessa Kirkpatrick
for their advice and help with the manuscript.

And thanks to the members of the writers' group
known as The Siding Poets –
Michele, Emma, Tom, John, Vanessa, Kathy and Craig –
for their encouragement and sensitive criticism.

The Wooden Gate
ISBN 978 1 76041 268 5
Copyright © Brendan Doyle 2017

First published 2017 by
GINNINDERRA PRESS
PO Box 3461 Port Adelaide 5015 Australia
www.ginninderrapress.com.au

Contents

Water lilies	7
Bridges	8
Three views	9
Treasure Island	10
Doyle's maxims	11
Please do not reply	12
Animal logic	13
Charity	14
Back to Basics	15
Morning	17
Gare du Nord	18
Tent embassy	19
This collection of atoms I call my self	20
Hanoi	21
Changes	22
The cut	23
Proverbial	24
Gaza	25
Aquarelle	26
France, Italia	27
Late August by the lake	29
Wind in the washing	30
My father's stopwatch	31
Coming home	32
Minerve	33
Prelude to a wet summer's day	34
Plagiarism	35
Everything's cheaper in Penrith	37
Devotion	38
The wooden gate	39

Anniversary	40
Winter gale	41
Not reading the signs	43
Airport, 11 September 2011	44
Spring is	45
Nancy of the bush drag show	46
Painted light	48
Broken wing	49
Ambience	50
Sublime Point	51
Last wishes	52
The heat's on	53
Bed of leaves	54
Babel	55
Nature study	57
Tribal	58
Piscean	59
This side of justice	60
Street dogs, Bhutan	61
Sky	62
Erik	63
Another day without my sister	64
Agnes	65

Water lilies

in memory of Marion Doyle 1951–2014

You left while it was still dark.
An angry wind
roared through the pines
giving way at dawn
to a swirling sky
of sun-fired clouds
like a theatrical opening
to paradise.

After the funeral
and days of cold and rain
the water lilies in my pond
seemed without life.

This morning
as I sat in contemplation
of light reaching the water
waiting
two flowers
opened
to the autumn sun.

Bridges

Eduardo showed me photographs
of him in the Guardia Civil
with his handsome moustache
on a bridge in Peru
holding a mortar
aimed at distant terrorists.

Eduardo has spent the night
at Fairfield hospital
with his sleepless little girl.
I love her so much,
he says with a sad smile.

Eduardo is learning English
to get a job as a security guard.
I see him now
in front of a bank
with his handsome moustache
thinking of his daughter
safe in her suburban home
and the weight of the mortar
and the bridge.

Three views

I walk the misty lane
a grandfather since dawn
thinking of Sendai
and another grandfather
searching for his lost precious ones
…
timeless
wondering
haven't you and I
been here before?
It all seems familiar
even this warm breath
on my face
even this
dim
airy
world
…
three kookaburras
splashing in the pond –
one for each of us:
me, my son,
my newborn grandson.

Treasure Island

Within our happy harbourside retreat
we celebrate a life that's rich and free
as round the barbie with our friends we meet
or watch the footy final on TV.

Our leaders stop the boats, turn back the tide
of those who seek to storm our country's gates,
to let them know that God's not on their side
nor will we ever count them as our mates.

The people smugglers cram them in the hold
of boats that are already overfull,
so join the queue, no need to bribe with gold,
and get a proper visa in Kabul.

Or if we must, illegals to prevent,
we'll just excise the whole damn continent.

Doyle's maxims

Sing for your supper. Howl for your dessert.

Always get up on the wrong side of the bed.

Don't gossip. Loose lips are too attractive.

Plant the seeds of discontent and water them daily.

Don't grow up. It stifles the imagination.

Try, try, then try to stop trying.

Don't eat your heart out. Become a vegetarian.

Don't tell anyone about your worst habits.

Pretend not to notice the dirt.

Take one disaster at a time.

Don't forgive bastards.

Never look a fascist in the muzzle.

Keep one foot in the grave.

Please do not reply

as this mailbox is not monitored
this is a message from the department of human services
you have a new centrelink letter available online
you should view your letter as soon as possible
by going to the inbox in your mygov account
if you do not have one you will need to create one first
by going to the website and then linking it to centrelink
or one of our express plus mobile apps
if you do not have an express plus mobile app
you can download one to your smart device
from the app store or google play ™
or the australian government department of human services
and logging on to centrelink services online
if you do not have an online google play™
app mobile smart device services account
call lifeline or the black dog institute
whichever you prefer

Animal logic

Does a bird think
I am bird
or a dog
I am dog?
Or does the bird
just live birdness,
the dog
dogness?
Does Jasper think
I feel sad?
No, he just stands there
dog-eared,
tail drooping,
attentive,
until the next
good thing happens
and wags his tail.

Charity

Twenty-five dollars a month.
Tax deductible?
Now you're talking.
To put a face on a smile,
yes, I did see it on TV,
in an African village.
A personal touch.
Yes, I'm sure we can afford it.

Oh, I have to write to them as well?
Maybe the kids can do that.
Good for show and tell.
A cheque will do?
Ah, direct debit from my account.
Excellent. That way,
I won't even have to think about it
any more.

Back to Basics

The Minister writes of Education,
'Historic Document' to the nation.
We parents wait, our breath a-bated.
What wisdom has the great man stated?

'What Our Students Learn At School'.
Ah, at last, here is the tool
That will unlock the mysteries dim
Of Learning, for our little Jim.

Will we be told of Curiosity
Or is that an out-of-date monstrosity?
Perhaps Love of Learning is his theme
Or Courage, Hope, and Self-esteem?

Will he invoke Jean-Jacques Rousseau,
Voltaire, Descartes, or Diderot?
Will he denounce Behaviourism,
Calling it a mental prison?

Perhaps Carl Rogers is the rage.
Jung or Illich may get a page.
Will he sing the Muse's praise
Or knowledge of the bygone days,

Or Scientific Revolution
To cut through all the world's confusion?
Will he treat with cool disdain
The calls for bringing back the cane,

Ensuring discipline comes about
From childhood passion for finding out?
Read on, I say, excitement stay!
What's Education for my child today?

'How to read. How to write. Mathematics.'

Ah, he has a pithy turn of phrase
This Minister of modern ways.
So succinct, yes, just the essence
Of what should be the children's lessons.

Let's not intellectualise
This Education, no, it's wise
Not to frighten Mum or Dad
Who want the best for girl or lad.

Yes, by gum, what more would need
Our children in this world of speed?
Back to basics, that's the shot,
All the rest is tommy rot!

Morning

The pond is stillness,
mind settled
like mist overnight.

Eyes closed, I listen to
dawn's birdsong
dance in treetops,

music of the bush
embracing all,
the many and the one.

A water lily will open soon.
Feeling her quiet presence
I say good morning
to my lost sister

just as she spoke
to our departed parents
each day at sunrise
and asked for their blessing.

Gare du Nord

Random lights of night's end
tattoo the dawn people
in the bar at the Gare du Nord,
crackling with neon wit
and last night's conquests
real or not.
Salut! says the barman with a wink
putting a friendly face
on the unborn day.

Twenty metres below
the people of the Métro snort and stir
in the plastic light.
Is the night not yet consumed
among the butts and bottles?

A lanky black gives his babe a cuddle.
An Arab looks sideways
and wipes his mouth
wondering perhaps
if the murky dawn above
will beat him home
to his sleeping wife.

Tent embassy

The dark ones laugh at us,
our heavy dance
and wobbly gait,
treading on stones
with tender feet,
feeding kangaroos by hand,
eating fish from cans.

But we know poison
and real estate,
the force of guns and laws.

Listen to their keening,
faint now,
for all the generations lost,
a halting corroboree
outside a defunct
white parliament.

This collection of atoms I call my self

(found poem)

All the carbon
iron
nitrogen
and other heavy elements
in our bodies
were made
inside
previous
generations
of stars

Hanoi

spatters of night rain
on Tue Tinh Street

a woman walks her bicycle
loaded with plastic bags

I watch her patiently sort
through rubbish

turn away from the streetlight
to pull out my money

find a suitable note
not too big

turn around
with inner generous smile

the woman and her bicycle
have dissolved into the dark rain

Changes

The lake's ruffled skin
twitches at the touch
of the north-west wind.

Nonchalant clouds hurry
over watercolour reeds and grasses
mottling the far shore,
so low I want to reach for them.

A raucous splash of cockatoos,
the wind changes,
darkening ripples
on the lake
where an old man drowned.

The cut

The years sneak away
like pups
through a hole in the fence.

'You have been profligate
with your talent'
said the successful playwright
but what of that now?

Looking at the death mask of regret
in a spotty mirror
I laugh
cutting my beard
and tossing the white hairs
to the winds of eternal change.

Proverbial

I want to leap before looking
I want to sow a whirlwind
and make hay while the moon shines
I want to gather moss with the Rolling Stones
and spend it all on a rainy day
I want to burn candles at both ends
I want to eat my cake and have it
I want to count my chickens before they've hatched
and put all my eggs in one basket
I want to bite the hand that feeds me
I want to drive a camel through a haystack
I want to see around corners
I want to cry over spilt milk

Gaza

Have you seen my friend?
We were playing football on the beach
a little while ago.
Is he hiding in the long dry grass
or in the empty shed?

Have you seen my brother?
Has he gone away with uncle?
Is he looking for food in the broken shop?
Is he playing where the bombs are
in the brown grass?

Have you seen my sister?
Mother says I must look after her
but I only went to get water
from the big hole
and when I came back
she was gone.
Maybe she went to Aunty's broken house.

There is smoke over the school
on the beach
and in the long grass.
Why is it so quiet?

Mother is calling for us.

Aquarelle

A delicacy of touch is needed,
but how delicate?
A sureness, a lightness,
transparency,
but how transparent?

You don't need glasses, says the teacher,
fuzzy is better. Turner was
almost blind in the end.

My watercolours today were disasters,
rubbing too hard,
even scratching the subtle surface.
You can wash it all off
and start again, he smiles.

As we said goodbye the other day,
brushing the softness of your lips,
tracing the smooth curve of your shoulder,
the colours started to flow again.

France, Italia

i. Le square Castan, Besançon

eighteen centuries ago
the Romans marked
their magnificence here
with a triumphal arch

this afternoon a drunk
pisses on a column
and his friend's poodle
shits on the mosaics

ii. Notre-Dame de Pitié, Remonot

'Bénédiction d'autos à 100 mètres'
announces the sign

there is a long queue at the chapel
and most drivers had parked
illegally on the narrow road

does the priest also absolve them
from parking fines?

iii. Militant

a young nun
crosses the square in Parma
quickly, gritting her teeth,
lips tight
brow straight

and the set look
I had seen before in Paris
except that she was selling
a Trotskyite newspaper
to the working class

Late August by the lake

Winter, won't you linger?
One measly snowfall is all you gave us
and the odd morning mantle of frost.
Your subtle palette of reeds and heather
too soon's upstaged
by precocious azalea and cherry blossom.
I look into the lake's mirror
and see no regrets.
It's been a cold one, the locals say.
I'm not convinced.
Winter's also in the mind.
Don't let these chirpy waterhens
chase you away.
Not yet.
Winter, won't you linger?

Wind in the washing

long jamies are in a flap over nothing
sheets snap, crinkle and pop
a lone business shirt puffs up importantly

bras fill with breaths
of air
a nightie suddenly gets flighty

at least the knickers aren't in knots
taut on top, loose below
long underwear does a jig

a black cocky shits
on a horizontal white towel
and a dozen long socks do a riverdance

pink hoodie looks askance
at grey tracky-dacks
not quite free of stains

chic long dress gets in a tangle
with a pair of jeans,
zipper slipping open

a button pops on a black blouse
and a row of T-shirts
rise to the occasion

My father's stopwatch

Along with photos of races won
it lies in a metal case he'd made himself.

I lift it gingerly, hesitate,
hit the steel button.
It springs into action
like a sprinter out of the blocks,

my father's stopwatch, a Heuer,
last handed fifty years ago
to a mate at Centennial Park
and he was off on a five-mile run.

With a shy smile he'd invite me
to pace him round the park
but a stitch soon sent me back
to catching tadpoles in the duck ponds.

I see him in some Elysian field,
sixteen years old,
running barefoot as he did
before he could afford sandshoes.

These last few mornings
I've been jogging on eucalypt-lined streets,
my heart racing
like his impatient watch.

Coming home

I was impatient to be back
here where mist weaves
about still-life eucalypts.
From the lookout,
dawn-soaked cloud
creeps along the valley.

To touch each day this wildness
as one touches a lover,
to hear torrents of skywater
somewhere
thundering, invisible.

Now rain fades,
roof creaks in the sun,
cicadas drone their summer welcome
and I am home.

Minerve

Two ancient rivers have gouged
crazed gorges in this limestone country
and high above, perched on a rocky promontory,
the village of Minerve, in late summer light,
blending into the garrigue,
pretending not to be there
in case other invaders should come.

Like Simon de Montfort eight hundred years ago
with his giant Crusader catapult
hurling destruction on the Cathar heretics
and burning them alive
in the name of king and cross.

We have the winding, stony
medieval streets to ourselves
and silence,
except for a woman's raucous laugh
from a wine-tasting bar.

We half-stumble down paths
worn smooth by centuries of pilgrims
and smile at the rusty council sign:
Rock Throwing Prohibited.

Prelude to a wet summer's day

Night frogs burp
their New Year's resolution:
I will try not to keep the guests awake.
Goldfish tiptoe
under lily leaves –
kookaburras still lurk.

Now rain is draining
from the watercolour sky,
wrung out of clouds
overstuffed
as Christmas puddings.

Plagiarism

In the beginning was the Word and
God created a host of golden daffodils let there
be light on the tiger and the lamb Little Jack
Horner sat in the forests of the night

it is a far far better thing all
men are created equal
in many-towered Camelot thou shalt
not commit adultery

born of the virgin Mary her fleece
was white as snow turned into
a pillar of salt where
will you go to my lovely

these things to be self-evident I have
a dream somewhere over the
rainbow what a piece of work
is hickory dickory dock

there's a place for us
here am I a stranger on a road less
travelled I'll never stop saying
Maria Juliet Angie Gloria Roxanne

follow the follow the follow the yellow
brick singin' in the raindrops keep falling
on my long beautiful hair Romeo wherefore art
thou she loves you exchanging glances

there are places I remember this
England wash that man right out of my
fee-fi-fo-fum I smell the move baby
move get in the jailhouse rock with me

no satisfaction in the town where I was
born things go better with (she don't like)
cocaine message in a bottle
I wrote it my way

Everything's cheaper in Penrith

And down we go for curtains,
mowers, petrol, boats and votes,
X-rated appliances, full-service repairs.
What mountain merchant can compete
on the level playing field
that starts at Emu Plains?

Do not envy us,
you flat-landers,
our pure air,
silence, stillness.
We have sandstone walls,
you have malls
and freedom of choice.

Go ahead, vote Liberal,
punish the chardonnay set
who left you in the lurch
of credit card debt and worse.
We will not abandon you.
The last station of our pilgrimage
will ever be Penrith
and our purses we gladly open
within your holy places.

Devotion

Huddled between mesh and glass
you rear up
gripping the silken sac
of your precious lineage.

I watch you weak from hunger,
obedient to nature,
snow-driven further
into a pitiful haven.

Days go by, uncertain,
you haven't moved.
Rescuer, I lift you and your treasure
to warmth, too late.

Unbearably light,
I place you on the pond
where priestly fish
complete the funeral rite.

The wooden gate

That week, we went to a kabuki show,
stories of wandering souls
in search of revenge, or lost love.

On my last night in Tokyo
my father comes in
at a wooden gate, wet with rain.

He looks at me with his hurt look
and says, I suppose it's not on here, then.
I've invited him to something

and haven't told him
the venue has changed.
I've let him down again,

my father,
dead these sixteen years.
How can I pacify his spirit?

After that I can't sleep,
and grey light dawns
over the grey city.

Anniversary

The pond is strewn with leaves
from yesterday's storms.
The water lilies
that bloomed so bright
are wearing black.

Across a pale sky
a lace of white cloud passes
indifferent as smoke.
Inside I light a candle,
kneel before its little flame,

breathe you quiet morning words
and search in vain
for that smiling photograph of you
to make a shrine

but it too is missing
in some untidy
attic room of loss.

Winter gale

Late April, I go down to the lake
thinking it could be
my last dip for the season,
step in, almost all the way
for a minute or so.

As dusk falls, I drive with friends past the lake.
A helicopter hovers over dark water,
a black swan beating frantic wings,
powerful eyes peering into the depths.
Rescue exercise, says our driver,
who knows these things.

We pass again, ten at night,
searchlights, divers.
A teenage boy has slipped
down into freezing depths
trying to retrieve something
as precious as a fish.

Two months on,
I'm drawn by a winter gale
to the lake, and a makeshift memorial
to the boy who loved fishing:
cricket bat, teddy bear,
a framed photo with his girlfriend.

Flowerpots have tumbled
in the unrelenting, indifferent wind.
Small waves on the lake
glint like scales
in the last of the sun.

Mikey Ryall, aged 16, drowned in Wentworth Falls Lake on 23 April 2014.

Not reading the signs

Some tracks aren't marked
with neat green signboards
leading you in a committee-approved
direction.

Some tracks are not on maps,
featured in guide books
or advertised in
Great Weekends Away,

aren't well-formed
according to an engineer's plan
designed on a computer
outsourced to a contractor.

Some tracks don't lead you
up a garden path,
to a monument,
or anywhere at all.

They may be scrubby and dark,
confusing, surprising,
forbidding even,
the ones you need to follow.

Airport, 11 September 2011

Cold towers of capital
wink in dawn smog.
Tastes a lot like coke,
says the machine on platform 2.
Vast streaks of pink and grey
over the gunmetal harbour
could win the Mosman art prize.

Ah, the airport, so clean, so upgraded, so
safe, even with all those foreign-
looking people walking around.

Explosives check, sir?
says the swarthy face
with cheesy politeness.
Sorry?
May we check your luggage for explosives?
Sure, I say, good idea.
We always ask your permission
of course.

Spring is

surge and urge,
change and danger,
instinct and daring,
the rising sap scoffing at mortality,

time's sudden leap ahead except in Queensland,
feeling older and younger,
the butt carelessly thrown
through the open window of possibility,

the magpie's patient toing and froing
to build a fragile incubator for its heirs,
the delicate intensity of earth's awakening
from winter's cold, compulsory sleep.

Spring is memories of youthfulness,
the high school Latin camp at Morpeth
with its bevy of cool classical beauties
and embarrassing plumbing leaks.

It's realising there's more to life
than mowing the long weeds
and the shock of a long black visitor
slithering by for a quiet drink,

and though winter showers poured
cold water on your dreams,
Spring warms the cockles of your courage
and all, again, seems achievable.

Nancy of the bush drag show

with apologies to A.B. Paterson

I had kept a blue French letter which I had for want of better
knowledge sent to where I knew him up the Cox's years ago.
He was stripping when I knew him so I sent the letter to him
just for the heck, addressed as follows: Nancy of the bush drag show.

And an answer came directed, though not quite what I'd expected,
(and I think the same was written with a plectrum dipped in tar).
'Twas his bass player who wrote it and verbatim I will quote it:
'Nancy's fucked off out past Dubbo in that rusty old pink car.'

In my mild erotic fancy visions come to me of Nancy
gone performing – what a trooper – where the clapped-out queens still go,
his mascaraed eyes are stinging as he flounces on stage singing,
for the drag queen's life has pleasures that the straight men never know.

And the bushmen want to meet him, they come up to him and greet him
in the murmur of old geezers as they hang around the bars,
and he sees the vision splendid of his contract being extended
and at night the chance to hook up with some veteran rock stars.

I am sitting in my dingy downtown office, where a stingy
monthly cheque's delivered from some tower tall,
and the foetid air and gritty of the dusty, dirty city
is recycled through the aircon spreading Legionnaire's over all.

And in place of lowing cattle, I can hear the fiendish rattle
of the suits and the stilettos making hurry down the streets,
and the language uninviting of the middle managers skiting
comes fitfully and faintly through the racket of their tweets.

And the hurrying people daunt me, and their botoxed faces haunt me
as they shoulder one another in their rush and nervous haste,
and their sunken eyes look seedy, anorexic shapes and weedy,
for day traders have no time to grow, they have no time to waste.

And I somehow rather fancy that I'd like to swap with Nancy,
like to pole-dance in a G-string as the punters come and go,
while he faced the round eternal of the cashbook and the journal,
but I doubt he'd suit the office, Nancy of the bush drag show.

Painted light

Walking down the track
into painted light
I'm like a kelpie
running after its master
open to discover the next moment
in the shimmer
of morning eucalypts.

All is as it should be,
all nature here
smiling
or benignly indifferent.

Broken wing

Morning, nature flashes
her avian jewellery
in slick swoops
and whoops of greeting.

A crimson rosella limps
like a veteran on my path,
turns in painful half-circle
like a busted wind-up toy.

My neighbour has a hospital box
– he's done this before –
throws a towel over its trembling.
Darkness will keep it calm.

Off to the vet.
It's the wing, she says,
so badly broken
we'll have to put her down.

I take myself home
empty-hearted, wondering,
when my wing is broken
will it be the hospital or the box?

Ambience

Making stately progress on the up track
your ears pop west of Linden
and sometime after Lawson
there's a change of mood in the quiet carriage:
taciturn Germans erupt to announce
they'll be doing the National Pass today.

Emerging at a higher station
you see every leaf and blossom in crystal light,
like a blind man touched by a holy hand
and know you're back home.

By your front door
the unweeded garden greets you
in nonchalant disarray.

Later, sitting in the quiet air
you hear a beetle whir,
a finch zings past,
rustle of summer leaves –
a rainbow is tasting your nectarines.

'Imagine standing on a scenic escarpment
and there's plane after plane roaring overhead.
It would certainly affect the ambience',
said the mayor in the local paper.

Now only the distant creep and clank
of a coal train on the down track
reminds you, briefly,
of the spreading cancer.

Sublime Point

I stood on a white cloud sea,
the rising sun projecting me
on a ghostly screen
in the chasm below.

A halo of rainbow hue
formed around my silhouette
which grew until, cloud ascending,
the image was consumed in vapour.

Three black cockatoos floated past
with funereal cry
as I and all the solid world
were drowned in white oblivion.

Now my haloed shape re-formed,
I moved my arms like a great bird.
They were angel wings
in time-lapse photography

until a cold mist enveloped me
and my rock, entirely.
Eyes closed, I breathed in the dawn
of a world born anew.

Last wishes

Nothing out of the box,
no need for an opera singer,
just a simple gathering around ashes
that could be scattered to the winds –
depending on the weather, of course,
I don't want to be sneezed at –
just a burnt offering to the ancestors,
though I don't expect anyone from Scotland.
You choose, dear boys.

Salmon Park in Newtown would be nice,
I used to play there,
if it's not high-rise units,
or La Perouse, where we almost became French,
or the duck pond at Centennial Park
where I caught tadpoles
while my father ran circles around me.
Or gently dropped in the Valley of the Waters –
or would I end up at the treatment plant? Oh well,
You choose, dear boys, you choose.

The heat's on

Insistent as a climate change denier,
it seems warm days will never cease.
We sweat and wait
for the cool caress of autumn
which isn't even on BOM's radar
let alone visible from their ivory satellite.

Impassive, Gaia valiantly turns on her axis
drifting through space,
waiting for a brighter species to evolve.
Our children nonchalantly tap their screens
in blithe amusement. We worry about our shares,
mortgages, school fees and paying off the overdraft.

Are you really tempted
to pass the buck to the engineers
and their big nasty space toy solutions?
Aluminium flakes for breakfast, anyone?

Lock the gate to the miners
and the doors on their masters
cosseted in the boardrooms,
methane issuing from their foul mouths
as the earth burns.

Bed of leaves

An almighty thump
of flight against glass
and a bronzewing lies on the path,
wings shivering like electric shock.
I sit on the bench.
She is turned towards me
with beseeching eyes.

I wait for her to recover, perhaps,
the brown head lifted at first
slowly nods forward
like a toy winding down.

She is giving up,
can no longer hold up that broken neck.
Now is still.

I approach quietly,
bend down to touch the intricate
warm soft feathers that carried her powerfully
into a false sky.

Hours later I return to a stiff shell,
eyes dull as stones,
gently lift her –
she has not left a trace of blood –
carry her into the bush,
place her on a bed of leaves
where she lies, beautiful
even in death.

Babel

Stop play listen stop rewind stop play listen curse,
take a break, look out of the tower over Lavender Bay,
Whiteley's house, glad not to have been him
but at least he'd followed his passion to the end,
while we were hooked on cheap beer at Kirribilli RSL
to wash down the Chinese.
Someone in Canberra had discovered multiple cultures
right under our noses
and decreed a special TV menu
to taste the various tongue dishes.
All we had to do was untwist the babble.

Reffos all we were, from Ukraine, Uruguay, China,
the Former This and That
or academic unemployment.
A team, we could translate you anything,
Lebanese soap, Polish puppet show, or Swedish sizzler
that had us hovering around the tall blonde's booth.

Beaming at our good luck
we beamed dull Albanian peasants
or scantily clad Scandies
into unsuspecting white suburban homes
across the wide white land.

We sold our word-talents by the foot from one-inch tape,
writing our gems in pencil on squared paper.
One of my first was Godard's *A Bout de Souffle*.
Jean Seberg's halting French took my breath away.

Some booths reeked of tobacco,
others of Chanel,
one of us a baroness no less.
We knew she was in when Rex was barking.

Years later, in underground caves in Artarmon
the digit went digital
and we scrawled actors' drawls
on the wall of a blinking screen,
bringing the world back home
to fewer and fewer viewers
until our masters said from now on
we must sell funeral plans and hamburgers
in the breaks between Hitler, sex and sport.

Nature study

Ring-tails
mating in the rhodos.
She watches me,
a bit anxious.
He's oblivious,
gripping her from behind,
slowly pumping away.
She suddenly looks
more nervous,
disengages,
jumps onto a higher branch.
He just sits there
looking dazed,
licking his privates.

Tribal

The flag was at half-mast on Hobart Town Hall.
It must have been sorrow, I thought,
for the sad life of Truganini,

who saw her mother stabbed to death by whalers;
whose sisters were kidnapped by sealers;
whose betrothed was thrown into the sea
by timber-getters who cut off his hands,
left him to drown
and raped his beloved;

whose brother was killed and stepmother
kidnapped by escaped convicts;
whose father died of a broken heart;
who worked as a guide and interpreter
for George Robinson, Protector of Aborigines –
he persuaded them to give up their land
while they died of disease and despair;

who turned to rebellion
and joined in attacks on white men;
who feared her body would be
mutilated by scientists after her death –
it was exhumed by the Royal Society of Tasmania
and her skeleton placed on public display.

I was mistaken. The lowered flag
was for an unlucky cricketer
from a white tribe far away.

Piscean

The glowing ball in the western sky
still well above the tallest eucalypts
patterns tea-coloured water

close to the familiar grassy bank of the lake.
I slide through the tingling cool,
look sideways for winged companions,
turn over into a leisurely backstroke,
follow the line of reeds past the hanging swamp.
Here a summer duck once shepherded three busy offspring,
wary of my large presence.

I stroke out to open water
and familiar cold heart-attack thoughts.
I'm mid-way on the big curve
that I hope will take me back
to my towel, clothes and car keys.

Attuned to the lake's calming hold,
with a breath of relief finally now in the same tea shallows
I gingerly touch bottom, wary of sharp sticks.
I step up out of the lake and hear laughter.
On the eastern shore young girls are doing somersaults,
tossing their long hair in the last of the golden light.

This side of justice

Paltry pickings, this side of justice.
Whitlam lived in Cabramatta, Turnbull on Point Piper.
Other times, other customs.
Meanwhile the harbour's deep as history:
one day the AMP tower will have wet feet –
but that's not Canberra's fault, is it?

We were the boat people
who brought guns, money and grog,
enough to destroy what went before and more.
Presto the trick was done,
blackfellas sucked in by sleight of hand
and the white ghosts
were masters of all they'd surveyed.

The rest is history. That is, the present.
Merchants arrive in jets,
buy up farms, vineyards, mines, water catchments.
Wealth alone gives them the right.
No arguing with zeroes
in offshore bank accounts, is there?

Street dogs, Bhutan

They're everywhere
as if they own the place.
There's one on your front door mat
and that last soft step
as you descend from the temple
has four legs and is snoring.

At dawn they play-fight as a warm-up to breakfast
then set off jauntily
along the road, part of the traffic.
By noon one lies in the middle of an intersection,
a living silent cop.

Afternoons they stroll in the hotel garden
or wait for leftovers in temple, monastery or back street
and at night bark their heads off
because they can.

Ignorant of chain or collar
these free-range buddhas
don't need to protect their patch.
They loll about all day in the sunshine
or curl up against the cold,
enjoying reincarnation
in the land of gross national happiness.

Sky

this still grey mountain
silence
augurs something
not to be found
in the weather forecast

something more fundamental
troubling
closer to heart and bone
a vision perhaps
of a self less perfect

something
now quietly weeping
from the sky
like grief
like a blessing

Erik

The old man has come to tell his friends.
In tweed jacket and woollen scarf
he walks slowly
through the tennis court gates,
head bowed against the cold wind.

Soon four men are around him,
one holds him close.
He mouths the unfamiliar words,
'I lost my wife this morning.'

He lets the men embrace him,
endures their softly spoken questions.
When did she die?
At home?
Was she ill for a long time?

The wind has ceased,
we thaw a little
in the winter sun.
Some of us go back to our game.

I look across later –
Erik holds a cup of coffee
one of the women has made for him.

Another day without my sister

In the bitter south-west wind
I feel our anger
at the months of your wasting,

in the depths of the pond
the morphined calm
of those last dragging hours,

in the slowness of sunrise
the gentle words we gave
to your closed eyes and twitching lips,

in the settling frost
the final heave of breath
that was your wordless farewell,

and in the pink-grey wisps of dawn
your love for living things
that we will hold within.

Agnes

in memory of my mother

I looked for a sign of you
that year, in Glasgow town,
walked the dusty Clydeside
empty as my longing almost despair,
not even a photograph or street address,
just 'near the Gallowgate'.

On a council estate
a distant cousin who was just a name
looked apologetic as he poured tea.
He wasn't even sure he'd ever met you.

The people's history museum showed
how you must have lived
and none of it looked gay or carefree.
The war had started
when you boarded a boat in 1940.
A rising pain in you
ended in leaving behind brother, parents,
and the grave of younger sister Marion
for a second chance at twenty-nine.

In a sandy suburb on Botany Bay
near the reeking cereal factory
you stayed with a cousin
and his wife from Lancashire,
found work and sunshine,
heard the bombing of Clydebank on the radio
and waited day after day for a letter
with news from home.

Five years you worked for a meagre wage
cleaning other people's houses
then, serving in a canteen at the airport
met a lithe athlete
with tousled fair hair,
shy smile, a fitter by trade.
He liked the look of you as well
and two late bloomers found love
and a post-war marriage.

*

With empty heart
I left the lively tourist town
you never knew
with nothing to show for it
except a poem.

Years later, in a photograph
that survived the fire you lit
in the dark wardrobe of the past,
you look out at me
smiling, calm, dressed for the honeymoon
with your handsome man, at last.

www.ingramcontent.com/pod-product-compliance
Lightning Source LLC
Chambersburg PA
CBHW062158100526
44589CB00014B/1865